ALLEN PHOTO

MW01055980

BOOTS, BANDAGES AND STUDS

CONTENTS

INTRODUCTION

As a sound and precautionary protective system, the vast choice of boots and bandages currently available could be considered a potentially valuable tool in your ongoing efforts to safeguard the health and wellbeing of your horse.

Throughout this text, it is not the intention to scare the reader into believing the ownership of a whole array of boots and bandages to be an essential prerequisite to any form of equestrian activity. Horses have evolved and survived in the wild for thousands of years without such protective aids, and it would be pretty arrogant of anyone to suggest that they cannot exist without them. Modern activities, both competitive and social, do, however, place unique pressures on the horse's constitution: activities that can be frequently exacerbated by their repetitive nature.

Ultimately, the use of boots and bandages all comes down to you making an informed judgement, based on an understanding of your own horse's abilities, an appreciation of his own particular traits, and an awareness of what products are currently available. Your horse's conformation, age and fitness level will, among other considerations, all have a bearing on your assessment of any likely risk. As an insurance policy against possible injury, current products and materials can allow the modern rider to feel a greater sense of confidence in the saddle than ever before, putting you in the enviable position of expecting the best, but being prepared for the worst, just in case!

LEG PROTECTION

BASIC NEEDS OF THE BUSY HORSE OWNER

Protecting your horse's legs, whether for competition, exercise or injury, requires a great deal of consideration; a reality borne out by the fact that developments in bandages and boots are more widely researched than any other area of horse equipment. New materials with high impact absorption, extra stretch and 'mouldability' are being developed and incorporated into boots (and some bandaging materials) continuously (*see page 7*). However, in a quest for the most protective or supportive boot, the busy horse owner has some very basic needs, which should not be overlooked:

- ease of application;

- speed of application;

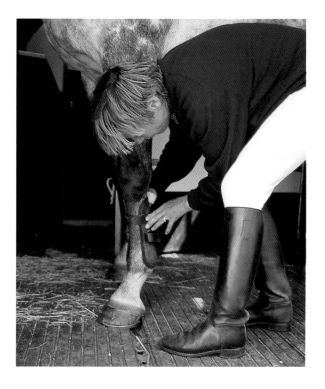

- security once in place;
- comfort for the horse;
- protection and support offered.

TYPES OF BOOT

BOOTS FOR RIDDEN WORK

When jumping or undertaking strenuous exercise, the practice of bandaging a horse's legs for protection against injury used to be considered essential, but nowadays it is more usual to see horses wearing protective boots. Boots are also worn for everyday exercise and schooling (*see above right*). In fact, it would now be more unusual to see a horse being ridden without boots than with them, as many riders use them as a general pre-cautionary measure against unforeseen knocks, stresses and strains.

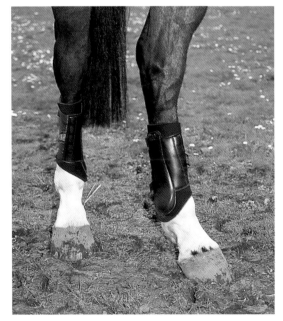

Brushing boots

Worn by the majority of horses for all kinds of ridden work, brushing boots provide a barrier between opposite fetlock joints because many horses rub these joints together when being ridden, an action known as 'brushing'. When fitted, it is the two boots, not the joints, that will rub against each other which prevents bruising and grazes. They should always be used on young horses being schooled or lunged as, often, youngsters cannot get their footsteps in order, and so brush until their movement becomes more rhythmical.

Brushing boots can be made of leather with a felt lining, although these have largely been superseded by boots made of synthetic materials which, having Velcro fastenings, are easier to fit, keep clean and do not absorb water. In order to offer maximum protection, most have a hardened shield on the inside of the leg. When correctly fitted, they should sit just below the fetlock joint on the inside of the leg and just above it on the outside. They should extend up the lower leg to a few inches below the knee or hock, although their exact positioning will depend on the boot's individual style, so the manufacturer's guidelines should be observed.

Speedicut boots
When a horse brushes badly, he may injure himself higher up the leg than normal, which is known as 'speedicutting'. In this case, a speedicut boot is used (*see right*). This is the same as a brushing boot on the lower half, but extends further up the inside of the lower leg until it reaches just under the knee or hock.

Fetlock boots
These are another variation on brushing boots and are used for the same purpose, on the hind legs. However, they are far shorter than standard brushing boots and only cover

Polo boots

These are very robust boots, designed to offer maximum protection during the tough sport of polo (*see below*). They are heavy-duty brushing boots which extend down and over the pastern and coronet, thus protecting the whole of the lower leg. It is crucial that they are fastened correctly as a loose boot can bring a horse down when he is travelling at great speeds, causing severe injury. They can be fastened with straps and buckles, with an additional strap fastening around the pastern to prevent them from flapping, or they can be bandaged into place. More often than not, they are both strapped and bandaged for a fail-safe system.

the joint, not the cannon bone, hence they are also known as ankle boots (*see above*).

Heel boots

These are used during particularly fast work (a game of polo for example) or when undertaking demanding jumping. They fit right around the lower leg, and cover it from just below the knee or hock, down to, and around the back of, the fetlock joint (*see below*). When fitted on the forelegs they will not only protect a horse from striking into himself with his hind shoes, but will also prevent injuries to the fetlocks and ergots should they come into contact with the ground, as can happen when a horse's limbs are at maximum stretch.

Tendon boots

Designed to support the tendon while the horse is undertaking strenuous work, tendon boots also protect a horse from striking into his own tendon: this is known as a high overreach. They can be open fronted or completely closed in depending on whether or not protection over fences is also required.

They usually, but do not always, have a protective shield running down the rear of the boot, which is often padded.

Shin boots

These are the reverse of a tendon boot in that the protective shield runs down the front of the leg to offer protection to the shins from knocks when jumping. However, tendon and shin boots are shaped differently so are not interchangeable.

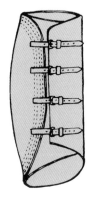

Yorkshire boots

These are most often used on young horses, who, owing to being uneven and unbalanced, 'brush' persistently. They are simply a rectangular piece of felt, or similar material, with a tape sewn right through the middle. This is then placed on the leg so that the tape is secured just above the fetlock joint. The upper half of the pad is then folded down, providing a double thickness of felt over the joint. They are deemed more suitable for horses who only brush lightly as they have no substance to protect against forceful pressure.

However, as they do not interfere with movement they leave a young horse free to develop his own natural action.

Anti-brushing rings

These narrow rubber rings fasten around the fetlock joint by means of a strap and buckle. Only one is used, on the leg most prone to injury. The idea is that the opposing leg will be prevented from rubbing against the injured one, thus allowing any injury to heal and preventing further injuries. In practice they do interfere with a horse's action and thus can cause stumbling, which in turn may present a vicious circle of brushing, stumbling, brushing. While they may be the only preventative measure to offer a solution to healing an injury in the short term (which would otherwise be rubbed by other forms of brushing boots), as soon as an injury has healed, other brushing boots should be employed.

Overreach boots

Often called bell boots because of their shape, overreach boots (*see opposite, above left*) fit over the hoof to protect the bulbs of the heel on the foreleg from being struck into by the hind shoe during fast work or jumping. They are commonly made of tough or ridged rubber and, less frequently, of leather, and either simply pull on over the hoof, or are fastened by means of buckles, straps and slots or Velcro fastenings. When buying a pair, make sure they are not so long that they drag on the ground as this can not only be extremely annoying for the horse but may also cause the boots to flip up.

Petal overreach boots are designed to overcome this problem of flipping-up during use (*see opposite, above right*). Instead of being a

continuous band of rubber, they have individual sections, running all the way around the hoof, which overlap each other. They make a peculiar noise when the horse is moving at speed, but are nonetheless very effective.

Skeleton knee pads
These lightweight knee boots prevent broken knees in the event of a fall when on the roads. They comprise a hard leather knee shield which is secured by an elasticated padded band strapped above the knee. Some have a lower strap but those which have no lower strap (so they do not interfere with movement) have a stiff construction around the knee shield which prevents them from flipping up during use.

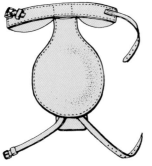

NEW MATERIALS

New materials with high-impact absorption, extra stretch and 'mouldability' are used in some of the most up-to-date boots on the market today.

An anatomic thermo gel made of cork paste and polyurethane gel (Veredus-Gel) is particularly sensitive to the heat generated by the limb; the heat moulds the gel to the contours of the horse's leg exactly, thus the boot also gives the kind of support normally provided by a bandage. The gel's cushioning properties absorb outside impact. The Event-Tec event boot (*see below*) has inside and front protection pads giving maximum

protection to tendons and ligaments should a horse hit a fixed obstacle, and has a three-way Velcro fastening to eliminate the need for over-taping. The boots are waterproofed by the PVC-coated neoprene cover.

Stomatex® (a patented product from Micro Thermal Systems) is a 'smart' fabric which has good stretching qualities and allows the limb to flex. This breathable material ensures the horse's skin temperature remains at a comfortable level by expelling excess heat and moisture through domes on the surface of the fabric. Pliable and flexible, the lightweight boots allow the horse to move without restriction. The Stretch & Flex Flatwork Boots (*see below*) combine the benefits of exercise bandages with the convenience of boots. They have a strong cushioned pad that protects the horse's fetlock joints and splint bones without hard rigidity, and have 'touch and stick' fastenings.

These new materials are fully washable.

BOOTS FOR TRAVELLING

All-in-one travelling boots

Today's all-in-one designs, protect the area from the coronet up to and over the knees and hocks (*see below*). They come in various materials, which are light and well padded. They are easily cleaned and comfortable for the horse to wear so, all in all, preparing horses for travelling is a relatively quick and simple task.

When a horse is bandaged for travelling (*see page 13*) you will need to fit additional protective items to the legs, which may include some, or all, of the following depending on your type of horsebox or trailer and the way your horse travels.

Knee boots and hock boots

These are used where shorter travelling boots (which only cover the area from the coronet to under the knee or hock joints) or bandages are fitted (*see opposite above*). They have blocked and padded joint shields that are surrounded by a felt or woollen material to provide solid protection from knocks during the journey. Each boot has two straps. One lies over a padded cuff above the joint and is

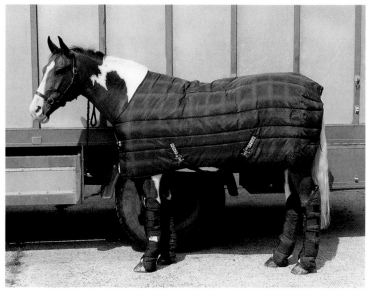

fastened securely but not so tightly that it would interfere with circulation (many have an elastic insert to combat overtightening). The other strap does up loosely below the joint as its only purpose is to prevent the whole thing from flapping about.

Coronet boots
These are like an overreach boot but are made of felt or leather (*see below*). They fit over the coronet and hoof to protect them

from injuries during travelling. However, overreach boots can be worn instead, on all four feet, and, if anything, offer better protection.

BOOTS FOR INJURY

There are various types of boot which have been designed for use in the treatment or management of injury.

Equiboots or Easyboots
Equiboots or Easyboots are ideally suited to keeping dressings in place, or for securing poultices onto the foot. The dressing or poultice is put on in the normal way and the

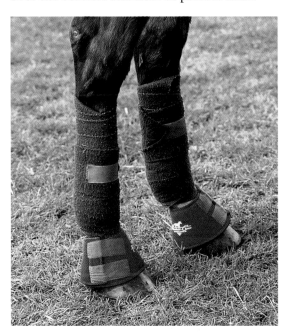

horse's foot is slipped into the boot which is then tightened up. The horse can walk about without getting the dressing dirty or wet, so there is the additional benefit that the horse can be turned out as usual. These boots are also the ideal solution for the horse prone to getting punctured soles while turned out in the field.

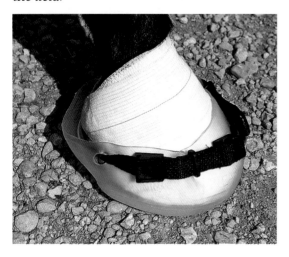

Poultice Boot

This is another veterinary boot designed to keep dressings or poultices in place but it is more like a Wellington boot in that the horse slips his whole leg in it. Poultice boots are ideal where the horse has injuries to his fetlock joints and coronet, rather than just his hooves.

Hose boots

These are like an exercise boot to which a hose can be attached. They save you from having to stand holding the hose on your horse's leg when cold hosing is recommended. You can simply fit the boot, turn on the hose and get on with grooming or some other chore while supervising your horse. People also come up with some clever ideas of their own; this photo (*see right*) shows how a hose-pipe has been wound around the legs to sprinkle water on them. Take care when using a device of this kind, some horses may not accept it.

Sausage boots

These boots prevent the horse from bruising his elbow with his shoe while lying in the stable or field, thus preventing capped elbows. They are thick padded rings of leather, which look like ring doughnuts and are fitted around

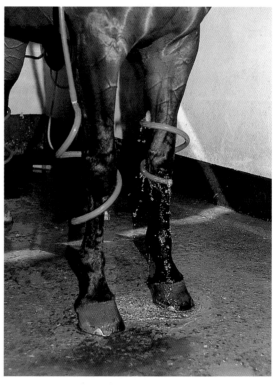

the fetlock by means of Velcro or a strap and buckle.

Cooling packs

There are many types of cooling pack, but they all have the same objective: to cool the leg and reduce swelling, thus offering pain relief. They are frozen until needed and then simply bandaged onto the injured leg to cool it. Make sure that the pack's outer covering will prevent ice burns. If you are unsure about this, bandage it on over the top of protective padding.

Equine chaps

The very first protective chaps for horses: Equi-Chaps (*see right*). These boots are made from the Stomatex® 'smart' fabric and reduce the risk of mud fever by keeping the legs clean, warm and mud free. They are designed to cover the hoof and go under the heel, and thus help prevent mud from getting up inside the chaps. The breathable quality of Stomatex® ensures the leg will not overheat and so the chaps can, therefore, be worn comfortably for up to twelve hours a day. A double layer of Stomatex® between the fetlock joint and the heel means that the chaps provide good protection against brushing and overreach injuries. They are also ideal for turnout and hacking because they allow full lower limb movement.

FITTING BOOTS

PREPARATION OF LEGS

Before you put any boots onto your horse's legs you must ensure they have been brushed free of any mud, dirt and grit and that they are dry. Any dirt or wet hair between the inside of the boot and the horse's skin may cause sores and abrasions.

FITTING TIPS

- Boots come in pairs and a front pair is usually shorter than a hind pair, often having one less strap.

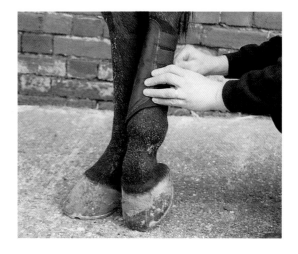

- Always ensure the straps lie on the outside of the leg and face backwards, except those of knee and hock boots, which face forwards.

- To prevent the boot from sliding down the leg if the horse moves, always do up the middle strap first to secure the boot before fastening the rest of the straps from the top down.

- Always use any keepers provided.

- Always keep Velcro fittings free from fluff and dirt, otherwise they will become less secure.

- Fasten boots tightly enough so that they will not slip, but not so tight that they will interfere with circulation. As with bandages, the pressure should be even all the way down and around the leg.

- When taking boots off, always work from the bottom upwards.

BANDAGES

BANDAGES FOR EXERCISE AND COMPETITION

Elasticated bandages

Traditionally, when elasticated bandages are applied for exercise, or on jumping horses, they have a layer of padding underneath (either gauze and cotton tissue [see below], foam filled pads [see right] or porter boots [see page 13]). However, there are now more modern alternatives in the form of elasticated, cushioned support bandages, which do not require padding underneath, but still provide protection from knocks, abrasions and strains.

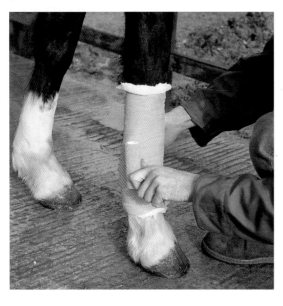

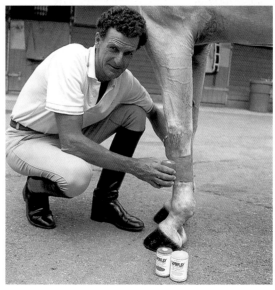

Elastic and cohesive bandages

For competition horses, bandages which provide an elastic fabric and cohesive system, give a consistent level of support throughout all gaits, moving with limb expansion and contraction but without the build up of pressure points (*see opposite, bottom right*).

PADDING FOR EXERCISE BANDAGES

Gel pads for use under saddles are now quite common, but by varying the mix of gel to latex, a high-impact absorption gel can be created, which is ideal as leg protector padding under exercise bandages. Such protector pads are extremely lightweight and are effective in preventing injuries caused by a horse striking into himself or hitting a fence across country. They also conform well to the contours of the horse's leg which, coupled with the absorption factor, helps in preventing the overtightening of bandages.

Porter boots

For exercise or competition, Porter boots (*see top right*) are also ideal for use as padding under bandages. They are made of expanded Plastizole, a lightweight close-cell solid foam that is moulded to the horse's leg. They do not absorb water so the leg protection does not become wet and heavy on a cross-country course and they will neither stretch nor shrink during use.

BANDAGES FOR STABLE OR TRAVELLING

Stable, or travelling, bandages extend from just under the knee to the coronet. They always have padding underneath, so the padding used needs to be long enough to cover this distance. You can now get special foam-filled padding (*see right*) which has rounded knee pads incorporated and these are excellent for added protection. Stable

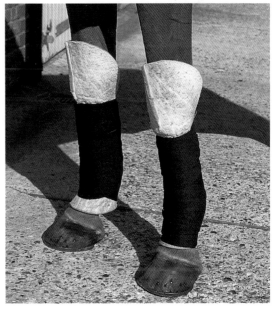

bandages are usually made of woollen material or stockinet and are used as protection when travelling horses, for the protection of injuries, or to keep filled legs down when horses are standing in their stables for long periods.

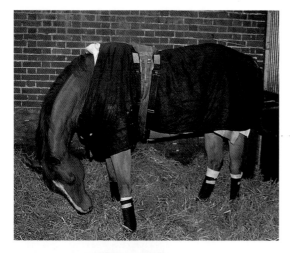

TAIL BANDAGES

Exercise bandages can also be used as tail bandages in order to lay the hair flat, producing a neat, streamlined appearance, or to prevent a horse from rubbing his tail when travelling. No padding is required.

BANDAGES FOR INJURY

Cohesive support bandages

Traditionally, when bandaging injuries it is common to use cohesive support bandages over dressings and poultices, however, unless you are experienced in using such bandages it is difficult to maintain a consistent pressure throughout. Modern cohesive adherent

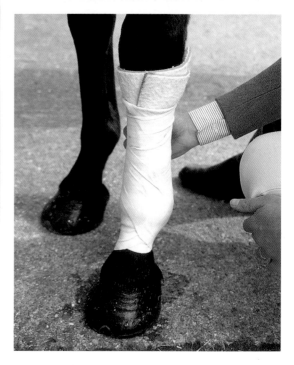

support bandages have been designed specifically for horses, to provide cushioned support and compression, without the risk of pressure increase after application. They really do hold dressings firmly in place but with a lower pressure than other elasticised bandages, making them very easy to apply at the correct tension. They are water repellent and allow the body to breathe, do not loosen over time and will not slip once applied.

Cold compression bandages and wraps

These offer a combination of cold and compression therapy in the treatment of swelling, inflammation and painful conditions of the muscles, tendons and ligaments. They are specifically designed to be soaked in water then frozen, yet they remain flexible enough to mould easily to the leg or joint. They freeze within ten minutes and are then applied to the affected area for fifteen minutes; after removal the area will remain cold for up to one hour. They contain no medication, are safe for repeated applications and can be used as a preventative aid for competition horses after a strenuous day. If your horse suffers from leg swelling, strains, sprains or bruising, these items should be an essential part of your first-aid kit.

SOAKING IT UP

Water absorption in boots and bandages is a point often overlooked. Having jumped into, or gone through, water, materials such as felt soak up water like a sponge, which results in your horse having to carry an extra pound of weight on each leg for the rest of the course!

APPLYING BANDAGES

BANDAGING PROCEDURE FOR EXERCISE BANDAGES

1. Make sure your horse's legs are thoroughly clean.

2. If using padding, cut a piece to the correct size so that it will cover from under the knee to just below the fetlock. If using cushioned bandages go to step four.

3. Wrap the padding around the leg so that it is firm and the open end lies on the outside of the leg facing backwards.

4. Unroll the bandage two to three inches then hold it on the leg just below the knee so that the loose end is free. Start to wind the bandage around the leg in the same direction as the padding (if used) until you have completed one whole turn. Then fold the free end down so that it will be covered the next time the bandage is wrapped around the leg. This prevents the bandage from working loose and coming undone at the top.

5. Carry on down the leg covering just over half the width of the bandage on each turn. It is important to achieve an even pressure all the way down the leg, i.e. not so tight that it will restrict the horse's circulation and not so loose that it will slip down. To do this, stretch the bandage to its limit and then let it come back to half stretch before applying.

6. When you reach the point just above the fetlock joint, start to work your way up again maintaining the same pressure. (Some modern bandages are applied around, and to just below, the fetlock joint, but this needs to be done with caution if it is not to affect the movement of the joint. It is more usual to see this technique applied when bandaging an injury [*see page 18*]). About an inch of padding should be seen below the last turn of the bandage.

7. Continue to work back up the leg. The aim is to finish about an inch from the top of the bandage. Take the tapes around the leg once (or twice if they are exceptionally long) ensuring you secure them with a bow on the outside of the leg, still maintaining an even pressure to prevent any pressure on the tendons. If you do the tapes up on the inside of the leg, the horse might rub them loose.

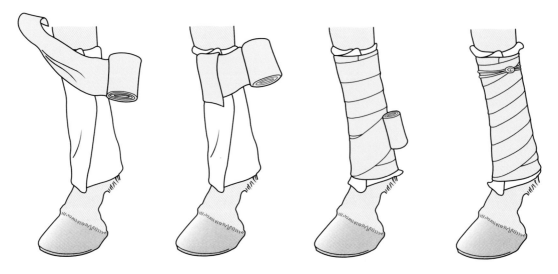

FASTENING THE TAPES

Tapes that become loose could be pulled or rubbed undone but there are various ways of preventing this. If the bandage is only to cover a dressing, then you can simply fold the turn of the bandage above the tapes down over them. If you are going to do any fast work or jumping it is sensible to protect them securely, either by using two full wraps of highly sticky tape or by sewing them.

BANDAGING PROCEDURE FOR STABLE OR TRAVELLING BANDAGES

1. Start the bandage in the same manner as the exercise bandage. Once you get to the fetlock joint carry on down to the coronet in a criss-cross fashion, working the bandage from the top down and then from the bottom up in a figure-of-eight fashion, so that you have an inverted V at the centre of the coronet, then work your way back up the leg and finish off as for an exercise bandage.

2. Many stable bandages have Velcro fastenings. These are safe providing the Velcro is cleared of any bits of fluff or straw. If the Velcro becomes clogged then it becomes less effective and the bandage could come undone.

3. If you bandage one leg because of an injury, always bandage the opposite leg as well. The horse will compensate for the bad leg by putting all his weight on to the good

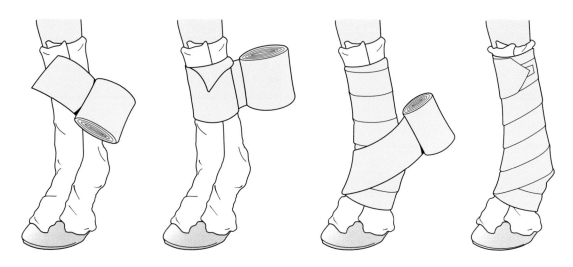

one, so a support bandage helps the good leg to withstand too much strain.

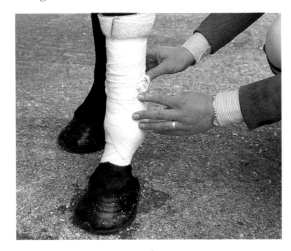

BANDAGING AWKWARD PLACES

Wounds may be in places where it is more difficult to keep a bandage on. For example, the forearm is a common site of injury but it is difficult to keep a dressing in place here. Once the wound is dressed, start by bandaging as for other leg bandages, but do not go below the top of the knee with the bandage (*see right centre*). Make sure the bandage is not too tight and that the pressure is even all the way down. The biggest problem with bandaging the forearm is preventing bandages from slipping down. Finish the bandaging procedure by securing the tapes on the outside of the leg as previously described. An Elastoplast strip may also be required around the upper part of the bandage to prevent it slipping (*see right below*), but ensure that the Elastoplast is no tighter than the bandage itself.

When bandaging knees and hocks, you need to use a figure-of-eight technique. Put plenty of padding around the joint, and bandage in place using a slightly elasticated or self-adhesive bandage. If bandaging the knee is done correctly, the bandage forms a cross at the front of the knee allowing movement and the back of knee is left uncovered, which still allows the knee to bend as normal. When bandaging the hock, do the same so

that the point of the hock is left uncovered (*see opposite*).

Tubigrip provides an excellent alternative when you need to secure a dressing in awkward areas, such as the knees or hocks (*see below*). It is pulled on like a stocking and can simply be folded up whilst changing the dressing and cleaning the wound and folded back down again once a clean dressing is in place. To enable movement of the joints, a gap can be cut out of the Tubigrip over prominent bones.

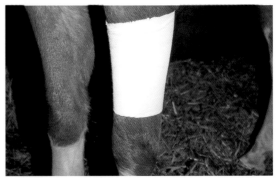

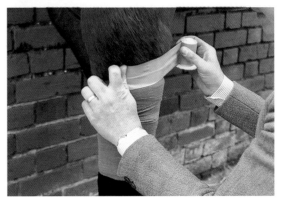

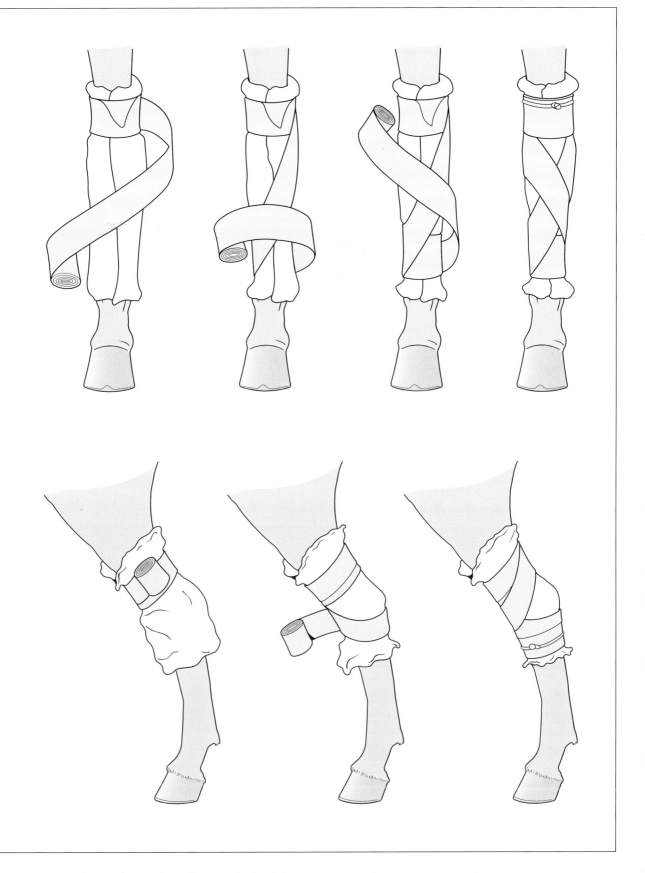

TAIL BANDAGING

When bandaging a tail no padding is required. Start at the very top, trying to ensure all loose hairs are tucked in. Work down the tail in the same way as when bandaging a leg, until you reach the end of the dock, then bandage back up the tail again. Fasten the tapes so that they sit on the outside of the tail.

To remove a tail bandage, do not unravel it all. Simply undo the tapes and slide it off downwards. This will make the tail hair lie flat, creating a good appearance.

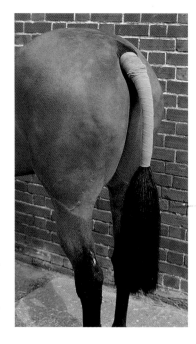

STUDS

There are two main reasons why your horse may need to be fitted with studs: either to prevent him from slipping on the roads, or to help him get a grip in less than ideal conditions during competitions. Whatever anyone might tell you, studs are not good for your horse's fetlock joints; they are, however, a necessary evil because without them you risk falling over in hard or slippery conditions, which could be far worse.

There is a great variety of shapes and sizes to choose from and most have a tungsten core for durability. Choosing the correct type of stud will depend upon the ground, the type of shoes in use and the activity in which your horse is participating. Generally, the harder the ground the more pointed the stud and the softer the ground the squarer the stud and, remember, perfect ground means no studs should be required. In reality, however, we rarely get perfect ground and, in any case, good going underfoot may be spoiled by wet, slippery grass, so, as many top riders will tell you, studs can make the difference between winning or losing a competition.

Many people put just one stud on the outside of each shoe. However, if you think about

this, one stud has got to drag one-sidedly on the horse's joints. When the stud sinks into the ground this pull is minimal, but what happens when the stud hits harder ground? Obviously the outside of the hoof is tipped upwards which affects the joints in the leg. Horses' fetlock joints have no lateral movement, so this tipping will unbalance and stress the leg. You might not notice any effects immediately as they will be minimal each time but, as these occurrences of stress stack up, two or three years down the line your horse may go lame as his leg finally 'gives up'.

To minimise any damage, it is preferable to use two studs on each foot, one either side, so a horse completely studded up will be wearing eight studs. If the ground is hard you might use studs with small points on the front feet and those with medium points on the hind feet. If the ground if soft you might use studs with fairly square points in front and those with large squares behind: remember, it is your horse's hind legs which are more likely to lose their footing. Furthermore, always ensure that you do not put studs into shoes which have worn thin. If you do it will result in the end of the stud driving into the wall of the hoof!

STUD GUARDS

When using pointed studs in the front feet, horses who snatch their front legs up tightly over a fence can 'stud' themselves behind the girth, so it may be necessary to use a stud guard or belly pad which attaches to the girth.

FITTING STUDS

1. The first step in the use of studs is having your farrier put stud holes into your horse's shoes. These should then be plugged as described on page 23.

2. Before putting in a stud you will need to remove this plug, so keep a horseshoe nail handy for doing so.

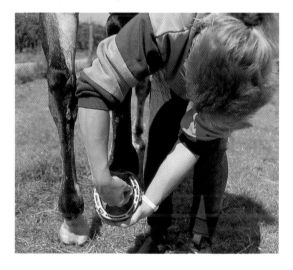

3. Place the stud tap into the holes and screw down to clean the thread and be careful to keep the tap square or else you will damage the thread. Do not allow your horse to put his foot down while you are using the tap otherwise he may panic at the feel of something attached to his foot and serious injury could result if he were to jump about or bolt (*see page 23*). Practise holding his foot up for some time, until you are sure he is quite happy about the procedure before using a tap.

4. While still holding the hoof up, select an appropriate stud and screw it in to the hole. Use the other end of the tap to make sure it is tight.

5. The type of studs you use in both front shoes must be the same, as must those used in both back shoes.

TYPES OF STUD

There are many different studs, although, for most activities, one of the following six will be used (*see diagram at top of page 23*):

- **Road studs** are for hacking out on the roads to provide grip and durability for the shoes.

- **Pointed jump studs** are for use in firm ground as they will penetrate the soil, offering hold without jarring the legs. They are ideal for all disciplines in such conditions, including dressage and showing.

- **Large jump studs** are longer than other studs and the end tapers off so that it will enter the ground more easily if it is slightly firm. They are usually used on the hind feet of horses undertaking demanding showjumping or cross-country courses.

- **Standard jump studs** provide extra grip in good going but when the conditions (perhaps dewy or rainy) might prove slippery.

- **Dome-top studs** are another long stud but they do not taper at the end, the end is dome shaped instead. They too are designed for demanding jumping, especially where maximum grip is required in soft going.

- **Sharp studs** have a round tapered barrel coming out of a square base. They are designed to penetrate hard ground, with the square base providing plenty of hold. They are used in all disciplines.

STUD REMOVAL

Having finished a competition you should always remove studs before putting your horse on to the lorry or walking him on to a hard surface. Travelling your horse home in studs is like expecting a man to stand on a train in stiletto heels.

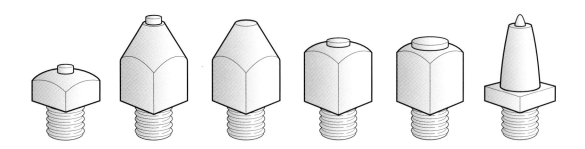

PROTECTION OF STUD HOLES

In order to prevent stud holes from becoming clogged with mud and becoming rusty, it is essential to pack them out immediately the stud is removed. You can do this by making a plug of cotton wool smeared in Vaseline (*see the plugged hole in the photo on page 21*), or you can buy purpose-made stud 'sleepers' to plug the holes. This photo shows the 'sleepers', plus the studs, tap, spanner and horseshoe nail. Make sure you push any plug right in (a horseshoe nail is an ideal tool for this job) and that it plugs the hole out right to the top.

INNOVATIVE STUD FITTING

For those who struggle with fitting studs or who have horses who fidget when studs are fitted, a new safety-inspired stud, tap and socket unit (STS) may be the answer to the problem (*see right*). The short ⅜th tap lessens the chance of penetrating the horse's sole or tapping too far into the shoe, and the flat unit lessens the chance of injury should the horse put his foot down. The sockets are located around the edge of the unit which is available in nylon or aluminium. Many people may find that the smooth, rounded shape of the unit is easier to get to grips with than the traditional spanner.

STUD CARE

When studs are not in use you should keep them wrapped in an oily rag and put them into a polythene box to prevent rusting, together with the stud tap, plugs and spare horseshoe nail so that they are all to hand when you need them.

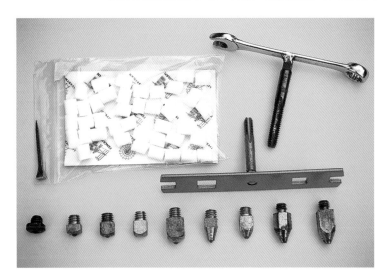

ACKNOWLEDGEMENTS

The author would like to thank the following people for permission to use their photographs: Bob Langrish – speedicut boots (page 4), hose-pipe device and Equiboot (page 10), porter boots (page 13), leg wraps (page 15 and stud kit (page 23); Alison Schwabe – Equiboot (page 9); and the following companies for supplying photographs and information.

Institute Veredus (Veredus-Gel products), Via La Valle, 50–51, 31010 MONFUMO (TV) – Italy. British Agent: Sue Taylor, The Lodge, 106 Langer Lane, Wingerworth, Chesterfield, Derbyshire, s40 2JJ. TEL: 01246 224777, FAX: 01246 224888

Equilibrium Products (Stretch & Flex and Equi-Chaps), 102 Hemp Lane, Wigginton, Tring, Herts., HP23 6HE. TEL: 01442 828228, FAX: 01442 828229

Flextol Ltd. (Flextol STS), Cottage Lane Industrial Estate, Broughton Astley, Leicestershire, LE9 6TU. TEL: 01455 285333, FAX: 01455 285238, E-mail: sales@flextol-ltd.demon.co.uk   Website: www.flextol.co.uk

Micro Thermal Systems (Stomatex®), Stomatex House, Bodmin Business Park, Launceston Road, Bodmin, Cornwall, PL31 2AR. TEL: 01208 79999, FAX: 01208 79990

British Library Cataloguing-in-Publication Data.
A catalogue record for this book is available from the British Library

ISBN 0.85131.815.0

Published in Great Britain in 2002 by
J. A. Allen an imprint of Robert Hale Ltd.,
Clerkenwell House, 45–47 Clerkenwell Green,
London EC1R 0HT

Reprinted 2003

Design and Typesetting by Paul Saunders
Series editor Jane Lake
Illustrations of bandages and studs by Rodney Paull
Colour processing by Tenon & Polert Colour Scanning Ltd., Hong Kong
Printed in Malta by Gutenberg Press Limited